ALEKSANDR ORLOV

PRESENTS

VASSILY

THE

KING OF ROCK

MEERKAT CLASSICS

RUSSIA 2012

Vassily the King of Rock
ALEKSANDR ORLOV

1 3 5 7 9 10 8 6 4 2

First published in 2012 by Ebury Press, an imprint of Ebury Publishing

A Random House Group company

Copyright © **compare**the**meerkat**.com 2012

comparethe**meerkat**.com has asserted its right to be identified as the author of this Work in accordance with the Copyright, Designs and Patents Act 1988

This is an advertisement feature on behalf of **compare**the**market**.com

comparethe**meerkat**.com and **compare**the**market**.com are trading names of BISL Limited

The Random House Group Limited Reg. No. 954009

Addresses for companies within the Random House Group can be found at www.randomhouse.co.uk

A CIP catalogue record for this book is available from the British Library

The Random House Group Limited supports The Forest Stewardship Council (FSC®), the leading international forest certification organisation. Our books carrying the FSC label are printed on FSC® certified paper. FSC is the only forest certification scheme endorsed by the leading environmental organisations, including Greenpeace. Our paper procurement policy can be found at www.randomhouse.co.uk/environment

MIX
Paper from responsible sources
FSC® C013123

Printed and bound in Italy by Graphicom SRL

ISBN 9780091949983

To buy books by your favourite authors and register for offers visit www.randomhouse.co.uk

This is a work of fiction. Names and characters are the product of the author's imagination and any resemblance to actual persons, living or dead, is entirely coincindental

A MESSAGE FROM THE AUTHOR

Please put your paws together for a brand new Meerkovo Tale – this time of superstar rock musician!

Some peoples think Vassily is just owner of tape cassette shop. Some peoples think he is just the trembly one trying to get relax in the corner of the Queasy Mongoose tavern.

But you don't get whiskers like that if you have sit at home all day dusting your slippers! Vassily has many secrets I think. Here we are exploring one of them.

If you know about popular music and rockings and rollings, you will understand where Vassily is comings from.

Please. Come with me into realm of noise and excitements.

Yours,

Aleksandr

ALEKSANDR ORLOV

**It was Midsummer's Day
and it was pouring with rains.**

In the middle of an enormous field, a group
of soggy meerkats were look up at the skies with
smiles of wryness and ruefulness. For today was
the first day of the famous Meerstock Festival,
and as day follow night that always seemed to
mean sogginess and damp.

At one end of the field was a stage of great
vastness. **All** around it there was much
scurrying as meerkat roadies moved lightings,
and drums, and speakermabobs.

They were all wearing rubber boots, and their tails were getting full of mud and wet, but they were all cheerful and excite as today was the biggest date in the rocking and rolling calendar, and all the most famous stars in the world were come there to make a lot of noise.

Roadie boots – being puddle tested to ensure the waterproof.

Over in one corner of field was long line of trailers. The first one was the biggest and blackest and was painted with big gold letters. "Vassily" it said on the front. And on the back, and on both sides. For this was most famous star of them all. Vassily, the King of Rock and Roll, and legend in his own life.

If we go inside we see Vassily himself, looking dark and dangerous in his black "Meertallica" t-shirt and his trademark black leather jacket. His crinkly face look like it has seen many late night.

He is surround by bowls of blue cheesy fleas and red beetle bits. (Vassily insist on having only blue cheesy fleas and red beetle bits. This make life very difficult for his assistant who has to paint each one blue or red).

As he sit crouch over his electric balalaika – it is very tense time before he go on stage, and he must practise his twiddly bits* – his mind take him back to the early days of his career...

*This is technical term, and mean the bits of songs with lots of twiddle.

Balalaika is ancient Russian triangular instrument.
This one is electricked for rocking and rolling.

Vassily had always been a shy little meerpup, who had a bit of stammer. The only thing that gave him pleasure was to play his grandfather's balalaika. After some years he got good at playing. Once he was even asked to play at the **Orlov** family mansion for **C**hristmas party. (Unfortunately he had attack of nerves and accidentally sliced his balalaika in half).

When he was bit older he was doing busking in Meerkovo Square. (Not for rich picking: Meerkovians are not flush with rouble). There he was discover by famous televisionmabob talent spotter. The talent spotter had sticky-up fur and a cruel grin, but he was very rich and powerful and gave Vassily recording deal; soon Vassily was doing headline at bigger and bigger rock concerts.

Doesn't the talent spotter look success and furry?
Perhaps his hat is full of rouble.

The famous Vassily Four Point Devil's Horn exercise
(for perfect paw presentation).

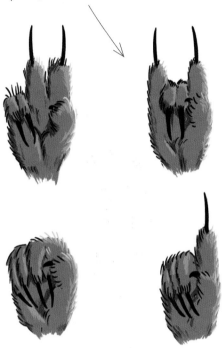

Meerstock was the biggest one of all. Vassily's was the last and biggest act, and he knew it was going to be seen by millions and millions of meerkats around the world. He was full of tension. (He was always suffer from nerves ever since his balalaika-slicing incident all those years ago).

Now it was time.

His roadies – who were all big and hairy and full of
muscle – come to lead him onto stage. Vassily clutch his favourite
electric balalaika with the flaming flames design. He had had a
cheesy flea and a small bottle of Meer Beer to calm him down.
He was ready.

See how giant is roadie?
I think you would not want
to mess with him!

The noise from the fans was deafen.

"Vass-i-ly! Vass-i-ly! Vass-i-ly!"
they shout as loud as they can, because they are
all very excite and want to see their hero.

What a fierce t-shirt!
(but I think we know Vassily
is not really so fierce).

Vassily climb stairs at back of stage. The light is blinding and the noise now incredibles. In middle of stage is great big meerkat skull with flamey eyes. Vassily is lift by electric platform up into the air.

He wobble a bit because the platform is very high up.*

*Vassily has always suffer from vertigo ever since he fell off the roof of Meerkovo School.

The opening drums roll... Vassily is terrified he open his mouth and nothing come out. Then he plays the first chord – and Vassily launch himself into his first song.

It is all right! His voice is work!

The crowd stamp and shout and roar – they are beside themselves with excitements.

Then he sing his all-time number-one hit, "Sympathy For The Weevil". The crowd go crazy and try to throw roses onto the stage and even some small items of clothing.

A meerfan – see the lovelight shine in her eyes!

As the lights go extra bright
he sing his famous thumpy-grindy
number – "Great Balls of Fur" –
and he feel he rocks. As he sings louder
and louder he worry a little bit that it
not just him who rock.

Whole stage is going bouncy bouncy.
But nothing matter. He close his eyes
in ecstasies; he is on a roll. The audience
cries louder and louder –

"Vass-i-ly!

Vass-i-ly!

Vass-i-ly!"

There was something about the voice that penetrate even the loud music. Vassily open his eyes. He find himself in his music shop, with his tape cassette on very, very loud – the machine is playing the recording he made for talent show. Now he sees it is me, Aleksandr Orlov, who is shout.

"Vassily! Turn it down!"

Vassily turn to tape machine that sit under gold disc which say 'Vassily' in big letters. He turn off music: his loud thumpy-grindy days may be over, and he may be bit deaf, but he has his memories.

Aleksandr's Life Lesson

If at first you don't succeed, then you must practise harder and more loud.

Now read my other greatest tales

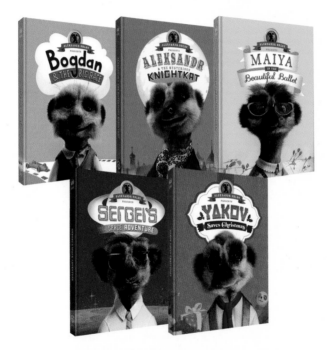

Available from all good bookshops

Also available to download as an ebookamabob
or audiomajig as read by the author – me!

For more information visit www.comparethemeerkat.com